BOOK OF GODS AND GRUDGES

D1520793

JESSICA L. WALSH

GLASS LYRE PRESS

Design & Layout: Steven Asmussen
Cover Art: Tyler Lastovich
Author Photo: Candy Bryant

Glass Lyre Press, LLC
P.O. Box 2693
Glenview, IL 60025
www.GlassLyrePress.com

BOOK OF GODS
AND GRUDGES

CONTENTS

I

II

III

IV

I

TRESPASSES

My first found kin were killers.
Both sides: a symmetry of mercenaries.
Some days I'm angry enough
to want the job and its benefits—
target, payment, blank space for motive.
Already I'm heavy with enemies
whose sins I can't remember
and some I never knew.
If an Indiana cousin comes today
I'll slam the door with the holy fury
entrusted to me by my mother,
who guards it for my gone grandmother.
I am loyal with anger. For love
I hate who my people hate.
My family's roots? Right there.

No Trees for Shade

In the last months, I brought to her
the man I would marry. She didn't know me anymore
but she'd remembered her lipstick.
She asked about his family, and promised
twice that *We are from good people.*
How hard she worked to believe herself
when we all knew our blood ran bitter.
Even when our people set out to make peace
they came home carrying heads.
Our people went to church with knives
in their boots, bodices, sleeves,
their giant unruly hair, and they rode away
on stolen horses they sold in the next town.
Our people didn't care about fine linen
unless it was time to bury their dead.
Our people kept going even then,
taking only their stories, a few true,
and the memory of the road they were on
when it came time to lay them down.
Our people were hard to love.
Every year it gets harder to keep track
of the toll and count of their sins.
Grandmother, I'm sorry
we are not from good people.
I carry from them blade, hymn, tale.
Let's bury the rest,
your white church gloves
marking the pile of sunburned dirt
beside an old Indiana road.

What Kind of Mother

At a Chinese restaurant in Michigan
my sister and I are kicking each other under a long table
while my dad and all the aunts and uncles talk serious.
Their voices are low and boring.
My dad says *Still, mom should've done something.*
She had to have known about Dad. Our house
was so small. She couldn't not know.

My youngest uncle changes the subject.
He's the one who almost became a fireman
but got kicked out because of drugs
which my sister and I know are scary things.
He talks about meeting an old firefighter
whose arms were quilted with burns and grafts,
whose worst memories were bodies just inside
unlocked doors, the near-survivors.
Smoke, the old firefighter had said, *sure,*
but sometimes panic.
You never know what you'll do
in a fire
till you're in it.
Once he heard a woman's dying screams
as she ran away from his help
to get her bathrobe.
She was a lady, I guess.
Had to be decent.

My dad and all the aunts and uncles
are never at a table again,
not all at once, and in her death
their mother is sainted
like a lady in a beautiful robe
dusted lightly with ashes.

In Collection

On a shelf in Grand Rapids
maybe there's a thick plastic bag
of tooth and bone, a bag of ash:

the remains of my grandfather,
whose six children gathered quietly
for what looked exactly like mourning.

They stood around a low-budget urn
my uncle had filled with kitty litter.
He said it feels the same.

He couldn't leave it empty but money's tight
and do you know what they charge.
Each said to the next *yeah, money's tight,*

maybe in a few months, and from that moment
no one spoke of him again.
He'd left his trailer to the daughter

he fucked the most
and she sold it for heroin, the biggest buy
she'd ever made.

When it was gone,
she licked the inside of the bag
until it opened at the seams.

BLOOD GUTTER

If Bubba has a real name it's Bubba.
When my body curves and bleeds, the same year
all the boys get rifles for their birthdays, it's time
for my first knife. I speak his name three times—
he's the guy, with signs at church and Bonser's.
My mother responds [quiet] then [sigh]
then *Jesus. Not Bubba. No fucking way.*
I took the kitchen knives there once, but you
couldn't see wall for confederate flags.
She pauses and says, *And other shit.*
Other shit is swastikas or klan flags.
She doesn't want me to be from a place
like the place I'm from. She curtains the words.
When my dad comes in, it's all *neverminds.*
Take mine—I can't imagine you'd need it.
We all imagine and don't say the words.

The Year of Confirmations

Me and God are on again the day we find the bird.
Heather's after Jesus and I'm after Heather. Ergo.
We pray over it because what better for broken wings.
It puffs and pants, smashes itself further into grass
and then in a twitch it dies. So we pray for it the other way.
Heather tells me not to cry because in Heaven
the wings will be whole again.
At the kitchen window, my mom is watching,
her cigarette smoke a cloud of irritation. She comes out
with a paper bag and says *Scared it to death, dincha.*
She laughs the way she laughs when nothing is funny.
With her bare hand she scoops up the bird, plops
it into the bag. She looks at Heather and takes a long drag.
Ashes to ashes, huh, and walks slow to the trash can.

You'll Be Disappointed

When she says *This is beneath you*
a single stalactite in my chest warms
and glows with *maybe*. At moments
I want to be good. Above.
But going high gets no one out of bed.
So I'm right back to black:
I'm a universe of hungry caverns
impossible to map. Whether toothed
or tooled, a creature in me mines
for darker dark, and I can't sleep
for the sounds of constant quarry.
I tunnel into myself ever further,
building cities to war with each other,
tending my sunless garden of grudges
with fertilizer made of acid and bones.
I was born on a low road. Nothing
is beneath me, I'm afraid. I go down forever.

AND THE PEARLY GATES ARE MADE OF TEETH

Whiskey-wrecked in a Kansas City bar
where an Irish punk band played
I shoved a skinhead with both hands
and yelled whatever you'd yell
if you were 19, drunk, and pissed off.

The fire alarm shrieked a second later
sending everyone into the quiet cold
of separate nights.
The way my friend tells it
the alarm was an act of God
but God, I want to finish it still.

I want to lose some teeth
but take more of his, to crack
a knuckle on his fragile temple. I was ready
to sacrifice, God. I believe
I am owed a debt of bones.

THE PAIN SCALE

I knew for a decade just one way to die—
the one that took my uncle, my cousin, all the kids
from my high school who didn't leave town.
I'd see them gaunt and purpled outside of the Wesco.
They'd call me Jennifer or Julie and ask for a five.
I heard I was the last person one guy talked to,
and I have never stopped knowing I killed him
with an embarrassed twenty and a good luck, man.
When my ex died in a wreck I said it every time:
No, his bike, an accident on his bike, like I could prove
another way to go young, like I could break a spell.

Fuck Marry Burn

All our parties are fires
on someone's cousin's property
at the end of unlit dirt roads
rutted deep from mudding

or that stretch of beach near the line
where town cops and the sheriff overlap
and neither ever bothers

Tonight's dark with clouds
The south wind confuses waves
until the lake doesn't know what to wreck

We've got a fifth of something flammable
and nowhere to be

Me I'm full of ghosts to burn
Hospital nights
That guy with the Mustang who wouldn't take me home
My 24th year from front to back
What I heard about myself when I knew I shouldn't listen
Bras that were never for me
Hours I spent using the wrong end of the pencil

Whatever you got babe
throw it in and watch

We all turn young in smoke

THIS SHORT LIST

I want to go back to 1987
and thank the men who didn't hurt me—

My father clutching a phone bill
grumbling about my calls
just to show me he had both eyes open.

Skater Aaron, the first boy
to call me beautiful, who waited daily
outside the school he skipped,
then begged me to tell him the story
of everything I'd learned.

My science teacher Mr. Craig
who brought in the heart
of November's first kill,
held it tenderly in two large hands
before offering us each a small piece.
Hold it in your mouth gently, he said,
this is how we thank the deer,
before moving onto dissection
because nothing was just one thing in our town.

I want to cut flesh from the hearts
of those men who didn't hurt me
and hold them beneath my tongue.
They are too few,
but their blood runs sweet inside me.

I want to go back to 1987
and spend no time or thought
on all the other men.
I want to leave their hearts on the ground.

BURNED COFFEE WITH THE HOSPITAL SOCIAL WORKER

What is it you understand

Are you shaking to wreck writing
but still drinking coffee
against sleep's thrumming failures

Are you cramping in half
running to the bathroom to lose
more that you could've consumed

Are you cracking your own teeth

Are you afraid to breathe deep
and make way for sobs

Are you unable to say it
like words summon it
like Candyman or Rumpelstiltskin
like the Devil
who you'd truck with
for a quiet night right now

Are you electrified
near the bathtub

What is it

CONTAMINATED

Earth's slightly non-spherical
its poles a little akimbo

On its surface once in Illinois
I held a woman's hand

while she cried about her man
her job her ungrateful kid

When she said she hoped for Trump
because everything would get better

I did not withdraw my hand
or demur even a little

All I could do was hold her hand
and I would hold it again

If I lose you here I lose you
like I lost a friend at Walmart

just by walking in the door
Lost another for skipping organics

If I lose you now I lose you
like I lost a poet over another poet

because one had done a bad deed
and the other swore sides

like I lost my neighbor
when I did not get a shelter dog

Stand far away
From a distance the Earth is perfect

Behavioral Health, 4:29 pm

Every waiting room is holy.

As for me I need a priest
or better still his Father

who can give me story and love
without love stories.

I need a sermon on a grievous sinner
given over to sacred strength,
the one voted least likely to turn saint.

Tell me of a grizzly haloed death.

Lately I see the appeal of martyrdom.
I'd trade these slowly clogging losses
for a zealous cause—
a burning building to run into,
a righteous war to die in.

How many heroics are suicides, God?
How long do I wait here?

OLD MATTRESS NOTWITHSTANDING

My lethargy of late is boundless
and infinite my ways of unaccomplishing.

I call in to say I don't feel well.
When did I last?

At most I'll wash the bras I won't wear,
scroll for supplements,

brush this interminable term's dust
from books I should and won't open.

I'd take to drink again but for the labor
of hangovers and a risk of recklessness:

Who is to say I wouldn't look straight
at the eclipsing world?

My bed is years beyond comfort or action.
I wait the days away.

WAIT I SAY

Whole rooms are made for it
designed to hold
what isn't happening

Wait on him   they say
Wait   they say   on him

as though wait is a verb
when we know it to be nemesis
a black hole contraction   action's inverse

Wait   I say   on what
reward   to what end   or ending

Remember grace   No
one deserves it
even the people who do

All we have   as we wait
is hope   that wait   some day   stops

Always the Door

I am my own guy from Porlock,
all interruption and sandwiches.
I lose track of what I've lost.
The sticky notes, layers of passwords and receipts,
like papier mâché over the frame
of something I meant to do.

In the unreal conditional
I would have shown promise.

Here, I am in my own way.

II

A Little Patch of Ground

Wasps lay claim to the wall by my desk.
I press my ear to sheetrock
and hear the muffled buzz of civilizations
or of my throat's alarm clock—
this time the stings would kill me.

It's a good time to be scared
but I can't muster fear when it's useful.
I waste it on garter snakes and mice,
the dark garage, a ball thrown my way.

I'm not scared of wasps
nor stings of wasps.
I don't want to die
but I don't try hard to live.
I keep no medicine with me,
never filled the prescription.
I could stop this right now
with a trip to the pharmacy
or a call to exterminators. I could stop this.

Not Mine to Give

Not that I care to please
but I dare myself to last

I know men
how they take and take

The option of survival
has never been

All I control
is the pace of my meting

Every prodded yes
yes it is killing me

but not quite yet

BEASTS AND CREEPING THINGS

I imagine Noah said *All set* and looked skyward,
in hopes of a pat on the head or a *Good boy*.

Below deck, creatures fought for space.
Above, clouds lumbered into position.

Surely in unrecorded truth many stayed behind,
a few overlooked but most by choice—

their world was set to disappear
and they so loved the world they stayed with it

where they nosed that night into burrows,
into nests and dens and lodges,

pressing into mates and offspring,
or alone, their flesh cradled by earth.

Wings closed over scales to hold the last warmth.
Something like a lion lay with something like a lamb.

As their time ended, they told stories of ancestors,
of love and battle. The spoke of why they stayed.

They knew the future was not for them,
and on the night of the first rains

they sighed that this was good, and this was good,
and all manner of things was good enough.

THE PURPOSE OF PRAYER

I shoot arrows to lose them
in hillside brambled grasses

to wade and rake and pace
seeking metallic stalks.

I shoot arrows to witness
as what I just held
camouflages against me.

I return with less.

I shoot arrows to count and cost loss.

At the end of every day
my empty quiver
sways against my hip.

One day fire will roll
from wood to prairie
and standing tall from char
will be frosted shafts
the stems of all I tried.

RELIQUARY

Being alive will be over
before I can speak of it.

As a child I played near the mill
and breathed deep the pines
loving trees and death of trees,
roots and needles, sawdust, sap.
I saw no border between wild and blade—
holy both.

Now, in funereal closets,
old boxes compress under new,
all holding pieces of pulse gone quiet:
photos of what's forever done,
wreathes and garlands,
baby clothes for my now-teenager—
even the vacuum's packed full
of lost hair and fallen crumbs,
squished beside summer jackets:
each a monument to a minute I lived.

WHY NOT THE TEMPLE

I am attached to my attachments.
I feed them like pets,
and to my own pet—
a small puppy—
to him too I am attached.

I say daily to my beloveds
I love you every day always
like a chant to save them
or a leash to hold them.

My love loops and repeats,
a hungry circle.

I am not worth your teachings,
Dorje Kelsang. I am failing you
and I'm doing it like a child,
my excuses part lies.

I do have time and a good car,
even money to donate,
soup to bring for others—

but I can't face you, Dorje,
to say my needs are unbeatable
and I'm not even trying anymore
to love anyone as much,
or love my loves less.

Pray for me, Dorje,
and know I tried a little:

just enough
to love you,
not enough to love all.

LIKE THE LAST ICE OF SPRING

On my first walk
since our sick winter
I circle the pond twice

When I come home
I say a swan is missing
from the pond's pair

My husband lets a silence stretch
I didn't want to tell you

To be like me
is a certain kind of fragile
not delicate but ridiculous

Once I was a fearless girl
clattering through lovers
and shattering bottles

Recovery shrank me
into a thick waisted woman
who jumps at small noises
and shakes at small changes

who can't handle the news
that a swan lost its mate

FOR THE RECORD

I say it must be coming for us
because I don't see it coming for us.
I look at the dog's picture from 3 years back
and find an old, old beast,
tired of carrying his loads of love.

He greys and whitens, mats and tufts.
How exhausted he is,
and how greedy I am not to see it,
urging him on and on to August
when he was ready that April, the same month
a doctor felt my husband's neck and paused
then pushed deep
finding tumor after tumor.

I look at my husband's picture and from here I see
swelling, the in and out push of cancer
that had grown for years, perhaps a decade,
but when I'd press my lips to his neck and linger,
I felt only desire, never disease.

Each day now I say *we are fine*.
Let the record show I believed it
and knew all along I was wrong.

THERAPIST'S PET

I spend my hours not knowing
what I want
or knowing what I need to want.

I say what earns a *good girl*
keep real problems
close and wrapped
like the whiskey on the tall shelf
with the glossy wax seal.

I spend my hours knowing
that I want to empty it down my throat—

but that is a bad want
and doesn't count.

I need to know what I need to want.
The sun is high and still
I know only *not this*.

Book of Numbers

The mathematical lie is x

My problem can't be solved
for treasure or emptiness
much less a number
  that wobbles on a cliff
    of less or more

How can this be soothing
  the seeking of equals
when not even one is one
  but possibly three   made of ones
    that defy census

God   I am trying to solve you
  inside all I've learned

      My husband won't write your name
          and if he's right
          if a word for you can't appear
              in my notebook
                the pretty one I bought
                    just for working on the problem of x
                    where x is your name unwritten
                then how do I begin

Let us say the stages of my faith are five
No
    that is grief
but the stages of grief are certainly not five

Let us solve for grief
  when x is the number of mirrors
    a mirror sees in itself
  when x is $y/0$
  when x is the number of things
    that didn't happen

The mathematical lie
is a graceless space
predictable   fair
where each side gives equally
  of itself
and no matter
  the steps   an answer

yes   just that
  an answer
looms

SELF-PORTRAIT AS THE LAKE

Neither loving nor indifferent to love

Veneered with *peaceful* at dawn

Dirty-fresh

Nudging shoreward
gifts of driftwood
and human feet
shoed but unbodied

Fickle and mum

Fury-churned when overflown

Cradling slow loyal beasts
who held on
from before
the age of scales

Gnashing through November
and each spring
rising

Greedy for oddities
and beautiful wreckage

Institutional History

In the second year
anatomists took my lake
and grew from it a coppery monster
who became my hideous haunted pet,
her eyes filled with bones,
her mouth thick with eyes.

At dawn I can see between her ribs
and I reach towards her
to stroke her riveted back into waking.
And on the windiest of mornings
when the long-gone lake would have spit tiny whitecaps,
I touch one finger to her sacred heart
to warm us both through.

Restructuring

The good go to ash like when Thanos snapped.
For the rest, like me, it's a wait-and-see.
How to name what I've accomplished?

Situation. Diorama. Circumstance.

I live through half-raptures, watch
as another's desk turns to office,
office to suite, their seat beside me empty.

I bloody my fingers trying to wipe my slate
but nothing about me comes clean,
and my scabbing hands send me further back.

All that I build-cut-carve amounts
to a state good people cross out of.

I have dabbled in being noble,
but those I boosted over walls don't pause to wave.
They leave me paper-piled and broke-banked.

My blank face in the right light could be pure.

LEDGER

Only half my journals are poems,
even those made of pretty cross-purposes

like waves weaving together
masking the deep current

that pulled down three girls
and returned only two a county south.

What I am saying is I have receipts.
You who owe me

favors, apologies, money,
thanks—

your name is here.
This is the book

in which I tally slights.
My memory once busied

with recipes & pick-up times
with deadlines & last menstrual cycles,

my memory lies idle
but for this recounting of wrongs.

What I cannot collect I herein speak to God,
who has never yet failed when it comes to reaping.

He Says I've Made Excuses

I made payments
        on four kinds of loans
I made a vow
        to worse & sickness
I made a fine CV
I made charming conversation
        with men on hiring committees
I made a secret bank account
        for vacations or divorce
I made myself wait
I made myself a shapeshifter
I made a girl
        then made a way for her
I made pillows
        out of old curtains
I made a perfect lemon cake
        brushed sugar glaze on it
        every 5 minutes until it glittered
I made a woman laugh
        in the last days of her life
I made room at my desk
        for crayons and paints
I made it farther than my grandmother
        though likely not as long
I made promises
I made it to the pharmacy today
        before it closed
I made much of little
        but not enough poetry

III

I Walk a Slow Mile

There was a time
when I lived whole days

neither in pain
nor in fear of pain

How did I hold that power
and not speak its name

How did I believe
I deserved it

What I had I didn't deserve
and I know that

because not once did I pray
my thanks   Not once

did I wonder why
I could run that strong

A young woman darts around me
and I want to say to her

There are pieces of today
we cannot deserve

Each time your foot leaves the ground
call thanks to fragile world

WHAT SOBER MEANS

Drunk is known unknowns
like Rumsfeld said
and I drank back then
so he was more and less
depending on the day's curve.

I don't try anymore to know
if I knew and didn't care
or didn't even know.

Even now in my coffee years
brick walls when I pass
still hold their breath
like I'll forever bring the shatter
and oh that glass music
of shards skittering down.

But the membrane's impermeable,
wormholes closed:
I can never have what I want.
Who I am in the morning
is who I am at dusk.

I am never at the quarry
in a Plymouth with a man
on the verge of something
that will change our luck.

I am never on the verge.

THREE SECRETS I SHOULD TELL MY HUSBAND

1.

The silver spoon of your mother's,
part of her family's set from the old country.
I ground it to scrap in her garbage disposal
then stuffed it deep in the trash. An accident
but I laughed because she hated me already
and I thought what harm, what harm can it do.

2.

Once I got in the car with a man who—
we're not doing that one.

3.

Today as the sun set over the lake
a hard and tired man on a motorcycle
rumbled slow past me, his radio
playing country music loud enough
for me to hear *guitar* and *beer* and *fire*.
He met my eyes and nodded
and I swear I would have left our life for him,
handed our furious teenager a $20 and my phone,
said *Call your father*, just split. Split.
I knew the joy already, felt my hair blow,
saw my arms wrapped around him.
I watched him ride on, hoping he would
and would not circle back.
Go, I would say. *Go*.

CALL IT SELF CARE

My therapist is forgetting maybe everything, surely me.
Today she forgets my daughter, then places her in college.
Gently I walk her back, watching her strain to know
what she knows. She gives me a handout she's given me before
and I take it like it's new. A year ago I came to pay someone
to pretend I am visible one hour a week. I wanted to be solid
in my body. I am tired, I said then, of pleasing and appeasing.
I am tired of smoothing. Now I sit on her small couch,
at times a stranger to her, at other times another client,
only occasionally myself. I keep coming and thank her every time.
When my benefits run out for the year I come anyway
worried that others will leave her, that she needs me.
I tell her I am feeling better. I am not. As for me,
it's easy, my own absence. It's familiar.
What I came to cure, I instead perfect. Find your calling, she says.

CATHEDRAL

When both door and window closed,
I tracked down my surrenders:
a drifting gentle mass, nation-sized,
gulled and rustling, made of needs.
Because everything I wanted, I got and threw out.

My neglected garbage clung tight together
forming for me an island, an empire.
Everything I wanted and got, I threw out
but it waited for me quietly
never doubting I would come.
The kindness. The calm. I come.

Its breezes reek until the breeze changes me
and soon the worst scent is my own human sweat.

I braid my hair with plastic bags
until I walk with a train of tentacles.

I bangle my wrists with cans
and the loops of a six-pack holder.

I eat from the meals I skipped
and though the gulls take their share
I will never run out of everything I wanted,
and got, and threw out.

At night I sleep in the nested center
wrapped in quilts of holey clothes.
The stars. The slow swell of broad waves.
The pieces of my trash interlaced.

Come noon I step from the edges
and swim the island's frilled shore.
From underwater, blades of sun slip
through pop bottles, bags, cd cases, papers—
through everything I wanted, got, and threw out—

all their colors ablaze and beautiful. Here then
is my good news: my garbage is stained glass
in the window of a cast-off church
and even here, only here, I can pray.

Mercy Emerges Imperfect

As if knowing how our tender faces
dulled by our endless breath
needed this day outside in sun

as if from thin windows
of papery rooms they watched whitening clouds
drag spring from long winter

as if they counted on our bodies
to pour onto lawns and paths
onto humble patios and fire escapes

wasps come crawling to share our light
not wanting to sting but stinging anyway
when we swat and spray them away

God how endlessly we want one without all
how deep our desire to cherry pick
when the cherry orchard's free of bees

How humble we feel when we ask
just this one day of unsuffering
how little we know suffering at all

Prayer at Half-Price Books

Lord, I tried to be good with my quotes,
scraped country from my tongue, penned opinions
on craft, theory, being. I dropped names—
even now they perch ready—and spoke codes,
ate small plates while playing just a bit dumber
than whoever wore the blazer. I've read them
all already, read them and still fallen.
The volumes of my days have changed.
Let a man size up my banana box
of books and pass me the value in cash.
I'll take what I can get, then spend it fast
on coffee and scratch-offs. Let's call it
communion, lord. Let's call this surrender.
The end of trying, it's being born again.

On the Pere Marquette

Fishermen prefer shadow, but fish, the light.
I've watched sunlight clamber down the tree line
into a dark river now glittering gold.
Hours of fishermen, in their slow casting walk,
have come along and then gone. A few wave
but most don't look away from the water,
their eyes reading the river's surface.

I wanted to see a salmon caught
and watch it wrestle free,
both parties victorious, both worse
for wear: fisherman proud and frustrated,
fish strengthened and scarred.
But morning holds back. Up in the cabin
I drink stove-burned coffee and wait
for something to learn. I watch a clock.

Out here I might need everyone
I came to get away from.
That's why I come. To go back.

Sand Made of Bones

When the rogue wave rose
    to its highest   rose to its utmost
shards of slate sheared off
  iced and graveled my spray-blind face

I knew an option must exist
but it was like a word forgotten
    when most needed   a sound skittering
loose   from others
  not the thing itself—

and when peak gave over to avalanche
    when the waters' plates slipped
  when all the earthy metaphors when they too withdrew
I knew then all I might have done

All the Small Festivals

In those years of light worry
even our music did little
besides giving us reason
to lie together in the sun
on blankets anchored by books
as we planned futures of poor joy.

When worldly stories broke through
they came ribboned with hope.
Nothing loomed.

We were content, I am saying,
with lovely abstractions.

A time happened and then,
one day, it ended.
The mystery is why.

Not every age is an apocalypse,
I promise. This one will end,
though the mystery is when.

MUST BE NICE

My parents said burnout is a luxury,
that people like us, we don't get to burn out--

and true, who chooses introspection
over car payments
or school clothes.

When I told my mother of our coming baby
she cried joyful tears but added
you don't get to find yourself once you have kids,
and a band tightened around my lungs
that has never yet loosened.

So what can I name this era of thickening,
of misery, when I wait until 9 to put on makeup
after morning's inevitable cry,
when I sit in my car outside work
like stones are piled in my lap.

I would call my old working parents
and tell them how I hurt enough
to carry a Bible,
download self-help podcasts,
how I tried yoga last week
and am thinking of sabbatical.

But I hear them already
between my jagged breaths,
their exhausted half-laughter.
Do you really think you can fall apart?
People like us—we don't.

IV

A Scale of Weed to Vine

Loose cigarette secret in the rain bad

Engine light and lost bad

Whole yellow pill bad

Put a star on days I don't eat bad

Sober coin tossed off a bridge bad

Breaking bottles on brick walls bad

Late for picking up my daughter bad

Search "how to disappear" bad

Dog shit indoors bad

Same shirt all week bad

I notice no one notices bad

Keep a poem going to stay alive bad

Stop and let it fail bad

And when at last my husband asks *How bad*

I say *It's fine Not that bad*

Only he knows I mean Nearly past bad

He reminds me we have been through worse

LIQUEFACTION

I've just turned 45. My genes
state I am halfway home.
My brain is shocked
to be alive. Tired, too,
of trying to be enough.

Today I learn my marrow's aged out,
the registry letter grateful
that I made myself available
in my vital time.

I tuck the letter in my purse
where I can touch it often,
this permission slip
to save no one.

My marrow, at least,
is useless to everyone but me.
It is all I can't offer.

Soon other parts will follow.
I'll go infertile, anemic,
get new knees or hips.
They'll pull my uterus out,
scar my breasts with biopsies.
I won't be able to lie flat on my back
and no man will want me to.
Piece by piece
I will be for myself.

On this day, right now

My father walked a block,
my daughter settled
a spat with her 7th grade friends,
my mother's foot has healed
though she cannot look at it,
and my husband's scars have calmed, lightened.
Our puppy sleeps, our furnace wakes.

In this space before the next need
what hums in me is—
what hums in me is nothing.

Is this when joy should come, when
blade and belt pause inches from my head
and I am not, for the moment, a maiden cut in half?

I try for gratitude, God, I do,
but I muster no more than quiet.

MINDFUL

Up early and cleaning
wondering what I took when   whether
it's helping   I step lightly
so they can sleep   Someone should
and I don't know how
Every time my husband says *relax* I cry

Since his sickness
sixteen people crooned *meditation*
I remember each one   and where and when
and I tried   to quiet this brain   to breathe
Is this breath right   too fast Is this air clean
Did I breathe like this
in the chairs outside surgery
while families came and went
One bench turned over four times   and I breathed
but how   Everyone was quiet
even when talking even the tv the phones   quiet
like waiting is a soundproof room
Is that stillness?

I've told seven people
my meditation isn't working
and they sad smug pity smile
tell me *keep trying*

My daughter age seven sobbed home
We were supposed to practice hiding
and be super quiet
because a bad guy could come
but I cried and so did other kids
and Ms. Eleanor said he'd find us

so shush   But we couldn't do it mama
Someone always made noise   I couldn't
stop crying   And he'd find us

Later when I walk out of yoga
person eight hears me say *My meditation*
doesn't take   She nods her empty head
  smiles her pity at me

I am halfway done
  with taking advice   The quiet
won't come   The noise
won't go   I'm not safe here
    lingering in panic

A day looms   I walk rooms
  winding my worries
like clocks

The baseboards gleam
when the first rays shine
My family   asleep
breathes low   and even

Nails Done

Above the ridge is the time before

I asked for rhinestones once
a skull on my middle finger
because *fuck the world* I'd say

before it fucked me up

I say money but it's not
Truth is I don't know that me
the one with pretty useless claws

Today I am the woman who
wakes up worried about mice
and crawls the floor with a flashlight

thinks of making muffins but doesn't
because who knows what we eat now and how

hopes for no calls

studies her husband's neck for swelling
and passes off the stares as love

My nails will grow out they tell me
and my hands will look
just like they used to

What was that? I wonder
I have filed the past away

Names for Middle Life

No one knows the close of an era, not when it happens.
Only later do we belt names and cinch them tight.
My past was a time of gliding when ease spilled freely,
became a river I floated down naked and un-sunscreened,
lulled by the smooth beauty of water, of my face in the water.
Like grace it ended suddenly with sheering of space and speed,
a quick coldness, a wintered glare in places that had been curtained
and a curtain drawn over every mirror.

Maybe if I could guess we'll call this my vampire time
when I swallow blood pills because I can't stomach meat.
I dodge cameras, direct sun, church, spices. My quivering
arms web themselves to my torso, and in any room
I am flapping, blind, and screeching. In any room I am trapped.

Or call it the *Incredibles* era when like the Mrs.
I knot and stretch beyond belief. My superpower is the absence of spine
and collagen. My superpower is returning to form and the kitchen,
where I make dinner and remind my daughter her choices are
disguise, defense, and disappearing—nothing else—because our
superpowers are all the ways of taking shit from men.

Or God willing it'll be called my Stepford age
when I seek mechanical reproduction. Even CGI is fine.
Let my husband not touch my placid duplicate instead.
Program her to smile tenderly, head cocked, cock-ready
even though he won't unless she's age-regressed. Make her easy.
Put her in her time of gliding and use her up.

Call this time whatever you want—just promise I won't know.
What I mean is let me out of time. I'm weary all the way through.

WHEN ALL THIS IS DONE

I want, I think, to be held together.
I want to be secured.
All my windows open on difficult clothing.
I say *sartorial*, search *couture*, type *bespoke*.

I shop for boots that lace to my thigh, leather
made of organic grass-grazing Italian cows
who sleep on waterbeds until they grew soft and large enough to kill.
I imagine wrapping myself in sacrifice.

I review email from a tailor who calls me Madame
tells me how to measure myself, since I must,
what a shame how we are reduced, isn't it,
but surely his corset dress will bring me love
and comfort me through these terrible times.

I consider lingerie that buckles together
in places I can barely reach on my own
or ties with silk threads too fine to be so strong,
everything crafted to do favors where I need them.

I have carts full, orders ready to finalize.
Somewhere a Frenchman waits on my waist,
and somewhere a nimble-fingered seamstress
pulls tight the stitches of a bodice I nearly bought.
A new calf moves into the barn stall emptied
for the boots I have messaged about, all but paid for.

I stay home, cycle two outfits, rarely bathe.
I loosen into cushions.
When asked, I say I am working.
I consider who I could be in the event of survival.

HARD-HEADED WOMAN

Somewhere in the cancer year,
my ironies depart
and I find myself in true love
with Elvis.

Even the yard sale bust—
hand-painted and fake-rhinestoned,
the one you held on the L
with that uncancered laughing body—
even he is dear to me now.

I dust him gently,
I caress him.
I consider a glaze
to protect his fragile blue,

wondering if the woman who made him
had in mind her Elvis moment,
maybe a concert or even a kiss.

Maybe she was where I am,
forever remembering what I missed.

Or did she simply choose sky,
the color of Heaven,
where surely she has met him by now?

I think of Heaven and I love it too,
and yes, I think of Elvis in Heaven.

I can barely remember
having time to mock love
or Elvis or Heaven.

We are here and gone.
I love you and I do it tender.

I sing no other songs.

THE HOLLOW

In truth   in bodily fact
  I gave up my heart for her
    carved and scooped   my center
left chest   the way we empty
    pumpkins when Hades pushes them
up to us   their orange blazing
    runway lights   for Persephone

I hollowed   then lined my ribs
    with mosses of the northern forests
      driftwood twigs worn smooth
  by inland seas   made a cradle
open to the sky   curtained with hair
I grew long and longer   and there
I placed her in the den of my chest

My neck grew crooked
  from looking at her   from days
    gathering grasses   trinkets
I could tuck around her

At night before we slept
  I unwove my tangled hair
from her fingers   then woke
to find her grasping it again

And when she grew   too large
  for my chest   when she clambered
    free   she lived there still
a small doll of herself   only
I can see

BETTER ONE // BETTER TWO

the bird in the tree // the bird with a leaf of the tree

the bed of the lake // the bed with a view of the lake

the sun through the blinds // the blind spot of sun with no blinds

your hair in the brush // the chair where she once brushed your hair

your hair left unbrushed // your hair in the mouth of a bird

a bird off to nest // her nest with a view of the lake

her bed by the lake // her bed where she sits while you now brush her hair

the sun on her bed // the sun on the nest she can see from her bed

your hair in the nest // the nest where the bird used a strand of your hair

the bed of the nest // the nest like the bed of a lake where you swam

the lake dried to dust // the dust on the chair where she sat as you swam

her hair in your brush // your bed like the leaf of a tree gone to dust

the tree in the dust // the sun on the nest made of strands of your grief

the grief of the sun // the blind spot of grief with no blinds

ACQUAINTED

I am alone and yes / I am in need and yes / I am blessed for reasons I don't
understand / no I am never quite grateful / these blessings are strangers
I greet with a nod but no smile / because I don't head for what's pretty
/ I know how many ways there are to die / and how soon / pretty is an
instant / gone before I can say its name in the mirror / every picture of it is
punishment / look what you had and didn't know / gone now along with
favor / gratitude like a photo is grief / I need no more of either / but I will
not turn away

IN HUMAN YEARS

We are dogs to gods
  who found us skinny and skittish in a city
fighting for garbage   meat
    a dank windless corner

Over and over
  we lick at their pity
follow them home
  cry for proper food

Some gods fear our kind
We are pit bulls to them
  passionate but quick to kill
  requiring attention
and they opt instead for cats
who are gods unto themselves

A god who loves a human
  shares chatter and contact
grows accustomed to our fingerprints
  learns to be precise
when issuing commands
  for we are such limited animals

  But no god makes life longer

We are young
and then gone

Is it comfort to know our god grieves
  when we die

The god swears
  no more not again
  I cannot stand it
and throws our things
  into wind river fire
  washes us from living planes

Is it comfort to know
gods are no smarter than we
  going back for more
    as soon as loss stops throbbing

We are irreplaceable
  to the divine

We are replaced

IF BY HAUNTED, YOU MEAN HELD

I woke to the dog's scratching
and for that half-sleeping second
it was the wrong dog, one long gone—
I expected him to be there at the door.

Each year the rooms of our house fill
with more of our lost loves: our families
whose imperfect arms held us up,
our friends, some reckless, some senseless,
our half dozen ill-trained dogs.

When I am afraid of next tests or new pains
I conjure our griefs crowding around us
not hungry ghosts but anxious ones
who cannot wait to touch us again.

ALL HER BONES ARE SCATTERED

My mother hated the soft coo
of mourning doves, set her jaw hard
when she heard them, flared her nostrils
like she would break their necks if she could.

Their call was the song of her locked room
in an old farmhouse, where once
a bat flew at her for what seemed like hours,
her mother adding time for each scream.
In the moments of pause, while the bat rested
and my mother quieted to a whimper,
the only sound was the mourning dove,
hooting like all was well.

For six decades, mourning doves cued the fury
my mother used to plug her tear ducts,
the sound of my grandmother's flint heart.

Today as we walk a flat, paved trail,
she tells me the mourning doves
don't bother her much anymore.
I think I've forgiven her, she says,
and when I look over to her
she seems smaller, ready to fall,
like forgiveness has drained her bones of marrow.

REUNION

The ratio of tributes to handshakes
tipped earlier than we'd imagined

At times we say *remind me*
and the list of what happened
is the list of all we loved

the lake the lake the river
a Ford truck
on gravel or mud
on open road with deer
or wild turkey
Wild Turkey

the lying frozen lake
the rip-currented outlet to the lake

When it's oxy or tar we say sickness
and talk about times we drank with them
at bonfires by the lake
or flying down dirt roads in the back of a pick-up

What we don't say
is we could all be here
every one of us

CONDITIONAL DIRECTIVES

If I die before R, trap me in amber, eyes open,
lined black, acrylics done to points, short skirt,
put me near the east window
so in the morning I glow him awake.
When you can, come and move me half an inch.
I need him to remember what's trapped can be freed.

If R goes first, lose me in space, gently push me away
so I never stop leaving, and make sure my curls are loose,
finally floating about me like the snakes they wanted
to become. As to all other matters, no matter. If I find
the end of it all, name the last line after me.

If I do it myself, and it would be pills, freeze me
in a jar next to W, a pack of cigarettes between us,
my drunk grandfather's Zippo from the war.
When we thaw we'll talk of how we burned through our lives
trying to stay alive, I'll tell him how I played joy after joy
for everyone, how fully I loved you, everyone.

WHEN MY DAUGHTER TELLS ME I WAS NEVER PUNK

I say, hon, my being alive is punk. I made my life
out of grudges when I saw the odds placed against me,

when my role was to marry a man who'd kill me
and give me my hot young death, a guy named Charles

who would have and nearly did—the day I said fuck you
and threw his keys in the snow? That was punk.

When I called a nice guy who'd loved me steady
and thought *what if I can try staying alive,* that was punk;

when I had my last drink and surrendered the scene, that too was punk,
and yes I miss the me who would be dead

because I was a bottle rocket, a pipe bomb of a good time
but my being alive is the middle finger I never put down—

I did not let these days go by, I clawed each one from dirt.
When I get my nails done I am cleaning weapons,

when I buy food, when I fill the tank,
I am threatening to survive long enough to piss off

a million awful people to be alive in spite of,
I am promising to stay flagrantly alive:

This is my beautiful house. I am this beautiful wife.
How did I get here? I say, *By my fucking teeth.*

NOTES

"Blood Gutter" is another term for the fuller or groove down a hunting knife, apocryphally believed to be a channel for blood.

"*Wait* I Say" takes its title from Psalm 27:14, which reads "Wait on the lord: be of good courage, and he shall strengthen thine heart: wait, I say, on the lord."

"Always the Door" contains mention of the "guy from Porlock." In his prefatory note to "Kubla Khan" by Samuel Taylor Coleridge, he claims he had composed several hundred lines of poetry in his mind during an opium dream, at which point "he was unfortunately called out by a person on business from Porlock, and detained by him above an hour, and on his return to his room, found, to his no small surprise and mortification, that though he still retained some vague and dim recollection of the general purport of the vision, yet, with the exception of some eight or ten scattered lines and images, all the rest had passed away like the images on the surface of a stream into which a stone had been cast."

"A Little Patch of Ground" is a phrase from *Hamlet* IV.4.17-19: "Truly to speak, and with no addition, / We go to gain a little patch of ground / That hath in it no profit but the name."

"Beasts and Creeping Things" references Genesis 6:20, which reads "Of fowls and birds according to their kinds, of beasts according to their kinds, of every creeping thing of the ground according to its kind—two of every sort shall come in with you, that they may be kept alive." The last lines refer to Julian of Norwich, who wrote "All shall be well, and all shall be well, and all manner of thing shall be well."

"Book of Numbers" is the name of the fourth book of the Bible and Torah. This poem is dedicated to Sarah Arthur.

"What Sober Means" references a speech during the build-up to the 2002 U.S. invasion of Iraq, in which Secretary of Defense Donald Rumsfeld said "Reports that say that something hasn't happened are always interesting to me, because as we know, there are known knowns; there are things we know we know. We also know there are known unknowns; that is to say we know there are some things we do not know. But there are also unknown unknowns—the ones we don't know we don't know."

"Liquefaction" is a process that occurs during earthquakes in which solids seem to lose form and stability.

"All Her Bones Are Scattered" is a phrase from Psalm 22:14: "I am poured out like water; and all my bones are scattered."

"When my daughter tells me I was never punk" includes references to the songs "Once in a Lifetime" by the Talking Heads and the Dropkick Murphys' "Middle Finger."

Acknowledgments

To Editor in Chief Ami Kaye and everyone at Glass Lyre who have placed their faith in my poems, I extend my true thanks. The world of poetry is better for your generous work.

I offer my gratitude to poets Lynn Melnick, Grace Bauer, Melissa Hassard, and Elizabeth Strauss Friedman, whose advice and support helped to shape this book.

Thank you to my family, especially my endlessly tough parents, for giving me the unconditional love they longed for in their own lives. To Robert and Stella, my favorites, for giving me joy and purpose; your love is my reason. To my people, that circle of friends who are my solace and safety. Your love is a glimpse of the kingdom.

Poems in this collection have appeared in the publications listed below. I thank the many wonderful editors who gave these pieces a way into the world.

"In Collection" *Ample Remains*
"Blood Gutter" *RHINO*
"And the Pearly Gates are Made of Teeth." *Passengers*
"The Pain Scale" and "Must Be Nice" *Lunch Ticket*
"This Short List" *The Walled Women Journal*
"Fuck Marry Burn," "Prayer at Half-Price Books," and "Sand Made of Bones" *Stirring*
"Behavioral Health, 4:29 pm" *Thimble Literary Magazine*
"Wait I Say" and "Why Not the Temple" *Amethyst Review*
"Reliquary" *Whale Road Review*
"Institutional History" *White Stag*
"Book of Numbers" *Psaltery and Lyre*
"Restructuring" and "Cathedral" *Five2One*
"He Says I've Made Excuses" *Glass: A Poetry Journal*
"What Sober Means" *Rock and Sling*

"Call It Self Care" *Fatal Flaw Lit*
"On the Pere Marquette" *Great Lakes Review*
"On this day, right now." *Without a Doubt: Poems Illustrating Faith*
"Nails Done" *Heartland Review*
"When All This is Done" *Rogue Agent*
"The Hollow" (as "Scraped") *Cotton Xenomorph*
"Better One // Better Two" *Bear Review*
"In Human Years" *Virga*
"Reunion" *SWWIM*
"When my daughter tells me I was never punk" *Nixes Mate*

About the Author

Jessica L. Walsh was born and raised in Ludington, Michigan. Her previous collections are *How to Break My Neck* and *The List of Last Tries*. She is a professor at Harper College in suburban Chicago, where she lives with her family.

Glass Lyre Press

exceptional works to replenish the spirit

Glass Lyre Press is an independent literary publisher interested in technically accomplished, stylistically distinct, and original work. Glass Lyre seeks diverse writers that possess a dynamic aesthetic and an ability to emotionally and intellectually engage a wide audience of readers.

Glass Lyre's vision is to connect the world through language and art. We hope to expand the scope of poetry and short fiction for the general reader through exceptionally well-written books, which evoke emotion, provide insight, and resonate with the human spirit.

Poetry Collections
Poetry Chapbooks
Select Short & Flash Fiction
Anthologies

www.GlassLyrePress.com

Made in the USA
Middletown, DE
23 August 2024

59051804R00060